D1527472

THE CHERNOBYL DISASTER

A History from Beginning to End

Copyright © 2021 by Hourly History.

All rights reserved.

Table of Contents

Introduction

On April 26, 1986, the worst nuclear disaster in history occurred at the Chernobyl Nuclear Power Plant in Pripyat, Ukraine, which was then part of the Soviet Union. On the surface, the disaster happened when a routine safety test of emergency operations went horribly wrong. In reality, there were institutional and internal problems that also helped bring about this terrible event.

To make matters worse, in the years after the accident, evidence was uncovered that the Ukrainian government and Soviet regulatory infrastructure were poorly equipped to handle the disaster. As the events unfolded, delays in response may have exacerbated the tragedy. Within days, the city of Pripyat had to be completely and permanently evacuated, the land, vegetation, and animals surrounding the power plant were destroyed.

The disaster at Chernobyl also had far-reaching political implications. This event occurred toward the end of the Cold War between the U.S. and its allies and the major communist powers, especially the Soviet Union. Chernobyl was an international embarrassment for the

Soviets, who looked inept and inferior. The later investigations into the tragedy only made things worse. What was more, the threat of nuclear weapons was an ever-present danger during the Cold War. It was a well-known fact that the Soviets had a substantial arsenal of nuclear weapons. If they couldn't keep nuclear power safe, what about those weapons?

Initial investigations into the accident showed that these fears were not entirely misplaced. The first international investigation concluded that improper safety procedures caused the disaster at Chernobyl. Mistakes made by nuclear officials at the plant that day led to the fire and meltdown. Later, a subsequent investigation revealed that it was actually a design flaw in the reactor that was ultimately responsible for the disaster, though poor safety practices discovered earlier exacerbated the problem.

As the Chernobyl disaster unfolded in the U.S.S.R., people around the world began to question the safety of nearby nuclear power plants. They saw footage of the people of Pripyat fleeing their homes, forced to leave most of their possessions behind. They also heard the fears from those who lived in other cities in proximity to Pripyat; even Kiev, the capital of Ukraine, was only about 100 kilometers (60 miles) away. Grassroots organizations (as well as organizations directly affiliated with the oil industry) lobbied for stricter regulations or even complete shutdown of nuclear power plants in the United States, Great Britain, and other countries globally.

Governments around the world responded, launching inquiries into the safety of nuclear power plants within their own jurisdictions. Some people had hoped previously that nuclear power would decrease the world's dependence on fossil fuels as a cleaner alternative. Those hopes were almost completely dashed after the events of April 26, 1986.

There remain many misconceptions about Chernobyl; in some ways, it has become the stuff of legends. This narrative will dispel those myths, but first, a thorough background of the Chernobyl Nuclear Power Plant is required for a complete picture of the events to come.

Chapter One

Background of the Chernobyl Disaster

"Nothing in life is to be feared, it is only to be understood. Now is the time to understand more, so that we may fear less."

—Marie Curie

In order to understand both the causes and impact of the Chernobyl Disaster, it is important to first examine the long history of nuclear energy, which began with the discovery of uranium in 1789 by a German chemist named Martin Heinrich Klaproth. It is a silvery-grey metallic substance that came to occupy the atomic number 92 on the periodic table of elements, as it has 92 protons and 92 electrons. However, uranium's radioactive uses and properties were not discovered until the nineteenth century; until that point, it was used primarily in early photography and as a colorant for ceramic items.

In 1896, a French scientist named Henri Becquerel discovered radioactivity through his work with uranium. Further research on radioactivity was conducted by Marie and Pierre Curie, and more discoveries about its uses continued to be uncovered, including in the medical field and for killing bacteria on food.

Throughout the first few decades of the twentieth century, scientists used better and better equipment to learn more and more about atoms, especially the nucleus of the atom, as well as radioactivity, fission, and related phenomena. Along the way, they discovered several new elements, further rounding out the periodic table of elements and helping scientists around the world accelerate their research by leaps and bounds. Much of this research occurred in Russia, where a nuclear physics program was founded in 1900.

One of the most important of these discoveries came in 1932 when a British scientist named James Chadwick announced the discovery of the neutron, a smaller, neutrally charged particle within the nucleus of the atom. At the same time, his peers around the world were experimenting with moving and manipulating the particles of atoms. Toward the end of the decade,

German scientists working under Niels Bohr (who had already made astounding discoveries in the fields of quantum physics and atomic science and won the Nobel Prize in 1922) successfully calculated the incredible amount of energy released through nuclear fission. That discovery is the foundation of both nuclear weapons and nuclear energy.

What happened next in the scientific field, as well as in the military and political worlds, is more well-known. As war raged in Europe and around the world in the late 1930s and early 1940s, scientists—many of them refugees from parts of German-occupied Europe—began looking in earnest at the possibility of weaponizing nuclear fission. One of the most important documents in this process was the Frisch-Peierls Memorandum, written by two German-Jewish scientists working in Britain. They hypothesized that a relatively small (5kg) amount of pure uranium would produce an explosion equal to the effect of thousands of tons of dynamite.

Over the course of the next several months, work on this theoretical weapon continued in earnest in Britain. Meanwhile, American scientists began paying more attention. President

Franklin D. Roosevelt authorized a nuclear program run by the army in October 1941, two months before the U.S. declared war on the Axis Powers. When the United States entered World War II after the Japanese attacked their naval base at Pearl Harbor in December of the same year, these scientists immediately brought the research before the military and high-level politicians. By early 1942, the construction of nuclear weapons intended for large-scale destruction was underway, under the secret code-name "Manhattan Project." It was chiefly run by the U.S. Army, but they worked closely with the British and Canadians.

What followed culminated in one of the most infamous events in modern history: the dropping of two atomic bombs on Japan, the first on August 6, 1945, on the city of Hiroshima and the second only three days later on Nagasaki. While both cities were home to important strategic military infrastructure, the bombs also killed hundreds of thousands of civilians and caused unspeakable damage. In the aftermath, people around the world were both in awe of and terrified by the incredible danger and power of these weapons. Their fears and horror increased over the years as more and more evidence came out of Japan regarding the long-lasting effects of radiation from the detonation of nuclear weapons.

Nonetheless, after the war ended, nuclear physicists turned their attention back to harnessing the power of this science for energy. In the process of developing nuclear weapons, scientists on both sides of the Iron Curtain (the U.S. and Soviet Union, and their respective allies) made enormous strides in the field in general. They had accelerated the use of nuclear energy by years, even decades, though at an enormous human cost. Throughout the 1950s, work began on the construction of nuclear energy facilities in the Soviet Union and around the world.

By the middle of the 1960s, nuclear power plants were either under construction or were operational in Belgium, Canada, France, Germany, Italy, the Soviet Union, Sweden, Switzerland, the United Kingdom, and the United States. By the 1970s, many more countries were added to that list. Scientists and politicians alike lauded nuclear energy for its environmentally friendly benefits (compared to the use of fossil fuels) and, most of all, reliability and safety. Eventually, Chernobyl would shatter that image.

Chapter Two

The Chernobyl Nuclear Power Plant

"Now, I am become death, the destroyer of worlds."

—Robert Oppenheimer, American scientist and father of the atomic bomb

The Chernobyl Nuclear Power Plant was by no means the first nuclear energy production site undertaken by the Soviet Union. In fact, by the time of its commissioning, there were already several others in use throughout the U.S.S.R. Construction on Chernobyl began in 1970 in a relatively remote, sparsely populated section of Ukraine about 100 kilometers (60 miles) north of Kiev. In order to operate the plant effectively, an entire town also had to be constructed to house the workers and their families. This was the town of Pripyat.

Originally, designers proposed to build the plant much closer to the city of Kiev. That way, delivery of power would obviously be simpler, and the government would not have to worry about where and how to house workers. At the time, nuclear power was considered abundantly safe, and the technology for using it was a source of significant pride for the Soviet government. It was even referred to globally as the "peaceful atom." However, the Ukrainian Academy of Sciences objected; even if there were only a remote chance of a meltdown, the risk, they believed, was too great to take in such a densely populated area. In retrospect, this decision probably saved many people's lives and prevented hundreds of millions of dollars in additional damage.

The Chernobyl Nuclear Power Plant was designed to house RBMK-1000 reactors. This model of reactor was exclusive to the Soviet Union, used graphite as a moderator, and had a somewhat atypical design and construction compared to reactors seen in other countries. This fact would become important in the aftermath of the disaster when people around the world began to question the safety of nuclear power.

The first of the reactors was completed and commissioned in 1977; the second in 1978; the third in 1981; and the fourth in 1983. Numbers 3 and 4 were a more modern RBMK-1000 model than 1 and 2. These reactors are also sometimes called blocks. Block five and block six were already under construction in 1986, and six more were also slated for a total of twelve reactors which were all to be completed and commissioned by 2010.

In terms of power, each of these blocks was capable of producing a massive amount of energy to the region and beyond. Each of the reactors could produce approximately 1,000 megawatts of electric power. Megawatts are used to measure the energy needs of entire cities, so this was an immensely powerful plant capable of powering well over 500,000 homes. At the time of the disaster, the Chernobyl Power Plant produced approximately 10% of all of the power consumed in Ukraine. That is an astounding amount of energy. It required about 6,000 workers at any given time to run the plant.

It is important to note that the disaster that occurred in April 1986 was not the first in Chernobyl's history. Nuclear accidents were not completely uncommon elsewhere, either. By the time of the Chernobyl Disaster, there had been at least eleven major meltdowns or crises at plants around the world, most of them in the United States. Major nuclear incidents are rated on the International Nuclear Event Scale (INES), which rates incidents on a scale from 0 to 7. Level 0 is categorized as a deviation, 1-3 are incidents, and 4-7 are accidents of increasing severity.

Before Chernobyl, there had been only one Level 6 accident, the Kyshtym Disaster in the Soviet Union. However, this serious accident occurred in 1957, and most scientists in the U.S.S.R. argued that by the 1970s, the technology had advanced so far that these sorts of disasters were no longer a threat. There had also been two Level 5 accidents; one took place in 1957 in the United Kingdom, while the other occurred in the United States in 1979 (the Three Mile Island Accident).

In 1982, reactor number 1 in Chernobyl suffered a partial meltdown, though this incident was kept secret and has not been rated on the INES scale. A faulty cooling valve in the core malfunctioned after routine maintenance, causing the tank to overheat and explode. To make matters worse, operators did not notice the leak until several hours later, which allowed radioactive material to escape into the air. Despite their negligence, no one was killed or seriously injured, and repairs were quietly conducted; it was years before news of this incident was reported, well after the 1986 disaster. The events surrounding this accident have been examined in relation to the disaster four years later. In retrospect, it was certainly an omen of things to come.

The world has only recently begun to learn about the next incident, which occurred in 1984 and affected reactors three and four. In April 2021, declassified KGB documents allowed historians a glimpse into what happened, though the actual events are still unclear at the time of this writing. Initial examinations reveal that the Soviet government may have known as early as 1983 that the Chernobyl plant was dangerous and should not have been kept in operation.

Just before the disaster occurred, the city of Pripyat had grown to nearly 50,000 residents, a significant number. The average age of those residents was 26, so it was a remarkably young city. In part, this was because so many young people worked in nuclear power. There were 18 residence halls in the town that housed up to 7,600 single men and women workers. In addition, many of the families in Pripyat were quite young. There were several thousand children attending one of twenty schools. Finally, Pripyat had a fully operational hospital, a public transportation system, and other features of a modern city.

In addition to housing, education, and infrastructure, there were a number of cultural and recreational facilities as well. Pripyat was home to several gymnasiums (including three indoor swimming pools), parks and playgrounds, a movie theatre, and a performance venue, the Palace of Culture Energetik. There were also multiple shopping malls, stores of all sorts, food markets, and restaurants. In short, Pripyat had become a comfortable, vibrant, and appealing place to live for young adults and families.

It is important to note that most of these families were woefully unaware of the incidents in recent years that signaled that a more large-scale disaster could be on the horizon at Chernobyl. At the end of April 1986, the residents of Pripyat, many of them also employees at the Chernobyl Nuclear Power Plant, went about their lives unsuspecting of impending disaster. Their lives were soon to be upended in what would quickly become the worst nuclear energy disaster to date.

Chapter Three

April 25-26: The Failed Safety Test

"We didn't know much about radiation. Even those who worked there had no idea. There was no water left in the trucks. Misha filled a cistern and we aimed the water at the top. Then those boys who died went up to the roof—Vashchik, Kolya and others, and Volodya Pravik . . . and I never saw them again."

—Grigori Khmel, firefighter

One of the greatest ironies about the Chernobyl Disaster is that it was caused by a routine safety test. In other words, it happened as its staff was actively engaged in preparing for just such an occurrence. Specifically, engineers were simulating how they would maintain cooling during an electrical power outage.

In the process of generating nuclear power, radioactive decay produces decay heat; unlike the heat produced by nuclear fission, decay heat does not stop immediately upon the reactor shutdown. In the event of an unexpected electrical power outage, the reactors themselves could be stopped relatively quickly, but since the nuclear decay would continue, scientists needed to find a way to keep the decay process cooled; if it overheated, it could cause the core to overheat or, in the worst-case scenario, to melt down.

Water is the best mechanism to cool nuclear reactors, but the problem was that the pumps that circulated the water that cooled the reactor (normal nuclear fission and decay heat) were electrically powered. Chernobyl was equipped with backup diesel generators to keep the water pumps running in the event of an electrical outage, but they took more than a minute to power on, which was a major safety risk. Even in that short time, the core could heat to a dangerous temperature. At the time of the disaster, scientists were working on other methods for cooling the core during that minute as well as trying to get the generators to function faster.

On April 26, they scheduled a test of this system. Engineers and scientists planned to turn off electrical power to the pumps in order to test the use of a steam turbine to power them for that crucial minute as the generators powered on. This was not the first time that the test was conducted. Engineers attempted similar tests in 1982, 1984, and 1985. On all three occasions, the turbine system proved insufficient to power the pumps long enough to keep the reactor cooled. After the failure in 1985, they made changes to the turbines and were once again ready to test them. It is important to note that on these previous three occasions, even though the turbine system failed, no accident or danger was presented.

In April 1986, there were several logistical issues and instances of human error that had not been present during previous tests. For one thing, the regulatory statutes surrounding a test of this nature did not require that all governing bodies be notified. Critically, neither the chief designer for the Chernobyl site nor the Soviet nuclear safety regulator was notified about the test. While they likely could have done little to prevent the accident, they may have allowed Chernobyl to better prepare for the chance of disaster and improved the immediate response during those critical hours after the initial failure. They may also have played a role in preventing one of the other key logistical causes of the meltdown, which involved a failure of another electrical power system in nearby Kiev minutes before the turbine test was supposed to take place at Chernobyl, and delayed that test.

Obviously, a great deal of planning went into what engineers knew would be a risky exercise. They planned to test the steam turbines at a time when the reactor was to be powered down in order to perform other tests and routine maintenance. Throughout the day on April 25, scientists planned to gradually reduce the reactor output to between 700 and 800 megawatts. This was considered a safer level for testing that would still simulate real-life scenarios. Once that level was reached, they planned to cut off electrical power to the pumps, power on the generators, and test the turbines to see if they could bridge the gap with the new changes in place. Once again, this test had been previously conducted and had failed in the past without causing any destruction, so there was no reason for them to believe that this time would be any different.

Everything was proceeding according to plan for the 14:15 scheduled test of the steam turbine until 14:00, when the accidental and unexpected power outage occurred at the plant in Kiev. The test was then delayed in order to avoid a shortage of power in the city during the afternoon and evening hours, peak times for energy usage. This meant that the scientists who had been preparing for the test all day, including the additional engineers on staff, went home for the day before the test was actually conducted. This, as well as other lapses in safety procedure, would later show investigators and historians that safety shortcuts were common at Chernobyl, especially on the day of the disaster.

The test had been planned to be conducted in large part by the day shift. The evening and night shift workers were only supposed to supervise safety procedures in the aftermath, which included maintaining emergency cooling systems while the regular cooling system as well as the reactor's capacity both came fully back online. Instead, the actual test was begun under the evening shift and completed by the night shift. It was not that these employees were unqualified to conduct this type of test, nor did they lack direction and leadership. In fact, Anatoly Dyatlov, the deputy chief engineer of the plant, was present and in charge at the time. Rather, they were unprepared that day, and the fact that two shift changes occurred during the course of the test left a great deal of room for communication problems and human error. All of these events helped lay the groundwork for the eventual tragedy that was to occur.

Shortly after midnight on April 26, the reactor reached an output level suitable for conducting the test (720 MW). However, the reactor cooled much slower than originally planned, in part due to the delay. What this meant was that certain byproducts of nuclear fission built up throughout those unexpected hours, causing what is known as reactor poisoning. These byproducts are ordinarily burned off during the course of normal operations, but because the reactor had been operating on reduced power, by midnight, the levels were becoming dangerous, and no one was monitoring them closely.

Next, the reactor experienced a sudden and unexpected drop in power. The cause of this drop is still unknown, though equipment failure or malfunction is the most likely cause, according to later investigations. The reactor was then reduced to a 30 MW output. It may seem counterintuitive that a near shutdown of the reactor would cause a crisis, but the reactor needed to maintain a minimum level of activity in order to burn off the radioactive materials it was still producing, particularly xenon-135.

In order to correct this, engineers and employees scrambled to return the reactor to a safer output level. In order to do so, they enacted several emergency procedures. While they were able to restore a safer output level, emergency signals in several important safety functions began to go off, and the entire plant scrambled to make repairs and prevent disaster. As the apparent crises piled up, Chernobyl staff had to prioritize where and how to respond. In an attempt to deal with what they perceived to be bigger problems, they ignored warnings about issues with the thermal-hydraulic systems. This decision would prove disastrous.

Despite all of these issues, the safety test went ahead a couple of hours later. Remember, the lowest recommended power output for the reactor, even during this test, was 700 MW. By 01:05, it had only reached 200 MW, but nonetheless, the decision to continue was made. The scientists and engineers now conducting the test increased water flow, which ostensibly should have made things safer, but because the reactor was so hot, the water nearly reached its boiling point, which is highly unsafe.

At the same time, the extra water flow did its job by cooling the reactor, once again dropping it well below recommended levels and even below marginally safe levels. The situation was precarious: on the one hand, hot water flowed around the reactor, threatening to boil. But the reactor was too cool and the increased water flow (though hot) was only cooling it faster. This meant that the plant accumulated dangerous levels of radioactive byproducts (especially xenon-135) very quickly. To make a bad situation even worse, workers had previously removed all but 18 of 211 control rods (which absorbed neutrons) from the reactor in an attempt to control the temperature and output. This meant that the automated system in place to shut down the reactor was disabled; it could only be performed manually.

In short, the reactor was extremely prone to crisis at this point. Despite the precariousness of the situation, though, workers commenced the originally planned safety test at 01:23. Several of these people died in the aftermath, but reports from others are unclear or mixed as to why the test was not called off.

Remember, the steam turbines only had to cool the reactor for less than a minute while the emergency shut-down procedures were initiated. This involved inserting all control rods into the core, which may have been commenced too soon. Regardless of why, the reactor experienced a spike in temperature, causing several of the rods to break. Within seconds, the power output jumped, and the situation became extremely dangerous.

The events that unfolded next had to be reconstructed primarily from scientific analysis, mathematical computations, and witness testimony as the reading and recording materials were destroyed. The last known reading of the reactor output was 30,000 thermal MW, though engineers estimate that it got much higher than that throughout the day. Undoubtedly, the jump in output caused a sharp rise in fuel temperature as well as steam pressure, which very likely caused the steam explosions.

The first steam explosion, as well as subsequent ones, caused massive damage to the reactor casing and cooling structures. This allowed nuclear materials to escape into the atmosphere and threaten everyone and everything around the plant. The second explosion, which was even stronger than the first, broke the nuclear chain reaction and exposed more of the reactor's interior. Fires broke out, and burning materials flew through the air, threatening other parts of the complex. The exact cause of this second explosion remains unknown. However, shortly thereafter, it was clear that reactor number 4 was critically damaged, and several parts of the plant were on fire.

There were other signs, even that day, that something was wrong. In the aftermath of the disaster, it became clear to inspectors that lapses in safety measures were not uncommon at Chernobyl. While it had no effect on the actual crisis that took place, the emergency core cooling system was left disabled for far too long a period of time on the same day as the disaster. Disabling it was part of another routine safety test, but the fact that it remained off for as long as it did sheds light on the crisis that unfolded simultaneously.

The coming hours would bring untold chaos and fear for the residents of Pripyat, and especially the employees who worked desperately to contain the disaster and prevent further contamination. At the same time, the world would become more aware in the next couple of days of the terrifying news of a nuclear meltdown.

Chapter Four

April 26-27: The Crisis Unfolds

"Comrades . . . Please keep calm and orderly in the process of this short-term evacuation."

—Portion of the evacuation announcement broadcast in Pripyat, April 27, 1986

After the accident and the initial explosions, the most pressing emergency was containing the fires that ignited as a result. Certainly, another major concern was the danger of nuclear contamination, but if the fire continued to destroy not only the reactors themselves but also the mechanisms that monitored and controlled them, all would be lost. Despite the immediate danger, though, the first firefighters on the scene were apparently under the impression that the fires were electrical in nature. They were unaware that the air and the debris around them could be contaminated.

The most dangerous fire was on the roof of reactor number 3, which was located next to reactor 4. Combustible materials were used in the construction of the roof, which ignited the dangerous blaze. The night shift chief wanted to shut down reactor number 3 immediately out of caution, but the chief engineer on staff at the time objected for unknown reasons. Operators were given masks and potassium iodide tablets (which can counter the immediate effects of radiation poisoning), and reactor 3 continued to operate until 05:00, around the time that the fire on the roof was finally extinguished.

The fire inside reactor 4, however, burned for days. Hundreds of pilots were employed in the days that followed to dump dirt, clay, and other materials intended to absorb some of the active neutrons and put out the fire. They, too, risked radiation exposure, usually without their knowledge. Whether or not these firefighters and pilots should have been told about the potential dangers would become an issue later during the investigations.

The effects of the accident were not only felt at the plant. Residents of Pripyat heard the explosions during the night, but it took a few hours more for them to begin to fall ill from radiation poisoning. The city was not immediately evacuated, largely because the town was governed by Ukraine but the plant was managed by the Soviet government in Moscow, and a communication breakdown caused the delay. Most residents of the city first realized something was wrong when they and their friends and neighbors felt the impact physically. By early morning, many people were experiencing a strong taste of metal in their mouths, a prickling sensation on their skin, severe coughing, crippling headaches, or persistent vomiting. By 05:00, when the fire on the roof of reactor 3 was out, it was evident to many that something was very wrong.

In large part, the lack of communication and direction led to widespread panic as residents of Pripyat trusted the government and plant officials to direct them. In the meantime, government officials scrambled and fumbled in their response. The massive Soviet bureaucracy meant that the news of the accident passed through several channels before anyone with authority to take action or evacuate the town arrived at Chernobyl. The biggest issue that caused the delay was the fact that while Chernobyl was located in Ukraine, the Soviet nuclear regulatory bodies in Moscow were in charge of the plant itself, but not the town.

It was not until much later in the day that the powers in charge established a formal commission to investigate the events unfolding at Chernobyl and in Pripyat. The commission was composed of high-ranking officials within the Institute of Atomic Energy, nuclear scientists and experts, and politicians. By the time they arrived in the area on the evening of April 26, two people were already dead and more than fifty others hospitalized. It quickly became apparent to the scientists and the others on the commission that the region was dangerously contaminated by the disaster in the reactor, which they deemed more than likely beyond repair even in those early days.

Finally, their investigations led to a full evacuation of Pripyat, which they announced in the early morning hours of April 27, a full day and a half after the initial explosion. Officials played an announcement throughout the town that provided basic information about what had happened and ordered an evacuation, which began around 14:00.

The evacuation order gave no indication that it could be permanent or even long-term. In fact, it expressly described the evacuation as temporary. This may have been because officials did not yet understand the scope of the damage or because they wanted to avoid panic while still getting people out quickly. The announcement asked people to bring only enough essentials for a couple of days, important documents, and some food. It stated that homes would be guarded during their absence. In large part, the residents of Pripyat complied, which is part of the reason why the town has the appearance of having been abandoned in a hurry—dirty dishes still in sinks, toys left on the floor, and other signs that its people expected to return home soon. The evacuation was only a minor step in what was to be a long, controversial, and difficult remediation process.

Chapter Five

Clean Up and Remediation

"There has been an accident at the Chernobyl Nuclear Power Plant. One of the nuclear reactors was damaged. The effects of the accident are being remedied. Assistance has been provided for any affected people. An investigative commission has been set up.

—Announcement read on Soviet television, April 28, 1986

It is very important to remember that the accident at Chernobyl had enormous public relations implications for the Soviet Union, still embroiled in the Cold War with the United States. It was partially for that reason that they did not immediately make information about what happened widely available. In addition, much of the inner workings of the Soviet government and its state agencies were shrouded in secrecy. When put in this context, it is not surprising that they were not initially forthcoming.

In fact, the Soviet Union only acknowledged the extent of the disaster after high radiation levels were detected at a nuclear power plant in Sweden, over 1,000 kilometers (620 miles) away from Chernobyl, on April 28. At that point, the international community became aware that something drastic had taken place and that the Soviet Union was in the middle of evacuating not only Pripyat but also other surrounding municipalities.

Other than securing the safety of people nearby and dealing with the international relations implications (discussed more fully in the next chapter), the officials within the nuclear regulatory agencies turned their attention to cleaning up. Their plan was to seal the damaged reactor inside a large concrete structure to prevent it from continuing to leak radioactive materials into the atmosphere. The first step to create this so-called sarcophagus was to clean up the debris caused by the explosions. This was no simple task, however, since the entire site was highly radioactive, and much of the debris was also contaminated, rendering the site and the area around it highly dangerous for humans.

An astounding 100 tons of debris was removed from the roof of the reactor and the surrounding areas, which would begin to allow them to build this containment structure. Because of the hazardous nature of this work, the government initially employed robots to do it. However, their parts failed quickly under the corrosive, destructive radioactivity in the air around them. At that point, the Soviet government felt they had no other choice but to use human labor.

Obviously, this was extremely dangerous work due to the radioactive particles in the air and on the debris itself. The laborers were drawn from the military and became dubbed "Chernobyl liquidators." Clothed in heavy, thick protective gear, they still could spend no more than 90 seconds on the roof of the reactor removing debris without risking lethal levels of contamination. Each Chernobyl liquidator was only supposed to perform this task once, with a constant stream of workers suiting up, taking iodine tablets, entering the zone, performing a small amount of work, and getting out. However, years later, many of the men involved reported being sent to do the removal multiple times.

Many of these people suffered health consequences down the road.

In fact, the disaster claimed many victims. Several of the firefighters who were among the first to respond died on the scene, while others lingered for days or months before succumbing to the effects of radiation exposure. Within the first three months after the accident, a total of 31 people died from acute radiation poisoning while 237 others suffered acute radiation sickness. Most of these individuals suffered from health complications for the rest of their lives, and many of them eventually succumbed.

It was imperative to the Soviet government and the rest of the world to construct the sarcophagus—the concrete structure that would encase the destroyed reactor—as quickly as possible because otherwise, radioactive particles and contaminants would only continue to spread. Wind carried the contaminated air very far distances. Rainfall also carried contaminants into water sources many kilometers away, putting thousands more people at risk. Animals also spread the radioactive particles. Birds, insects, and any other creatures—particularly those who flew—carried the contaminants on their bodies with them wherever they went after landing at the Chernobyl site.

Construction of the sarcophagus began in early June 1986 and lasted until November. Clearly, the biggest challenge was protecting the crew from exposure to radiation. Steps such as building construction equipment with lead cabins and continuously rotating workers in heavy protective gear slowed the project considerably. Nonetheless, crews worked tirelessly and diligently to protect the surrounding area and encase the reactor as quickly as possible.

Over time, radioactive materials naturally decay, rendering them virtually harmless. However, the Soviet government and the regulatory commissions decided that they could not wait for nature to take care of the clean-up. They felt strongly that, while Pripyat would likely not be inhabitable again, other surrounding towns and cities needed to be usable. Even more crucially, the land in the surrounding region needed to be available for cultivation. Therefore, they made concerted attempts at remediation in these places.

Chernobyl liquidators set to work at a myriad of tasks, including washing buildings, structures, and streets, and removing contaminated objects.

They also brought soil and plants in from other regions to replace contaminated dirt and earth and took other steps to make the land livable again. Once again, many of the liquidation workers were exposed to unsafe levels of radiation and suffered long-term consequences.

Some historians believe that these efforts were more about public relations and confidence in nuclear energy and nuclear programs than actual remediation. The Soviet government feared that if a large area around the Chernobyl Nuclear Power Plant were to be rendered unusable or unlivable for too long, many people would come to fear nuclear energy and reject it. If the remediation from a disaster as large as the one in Chernobyl could be handled neatly and quickly, then the people in power surmised that the public would be more comfortable with nuclear energy.

Another major concern, even after the crews completed construction of the sarcophagus, was the condition of what remained of the reactor and all of the contaminated material inside. There were real fears that there could be another explosion that would break through the concrete encasement. Therefore, scientists continued to monitor what was taking place inside as best they could. They also removed as many of the remaining rods as possible from inside the reactor. Both in the process of removing them and monitoring the activity inside, several more people became exposed to radiation and experienced the effects of radiation poisoning. It may seem that this fact has been repeated multiple times, but it is important to emphasize the human toll of the Chernobyl disaster.

By the end of 1986, these scientists were finally able to conclude that the reactor that had caused so much chaos, destruction, sickness, and death was no longer a threat. With this finding and the sarcophagus construction also complete, the Soviet Union and the world turned their attention to the investigations into what had actually occurred that fateful day in April.

Chapter Six

The World Responds

"The accident at the Chernobyl nuclear plant has painfully affected the Soviet people and shocked the international community. For the first time, we confront the real force of nuclear energy, out of control."

—Mikhail Gorbachev

As the Soviet and Ukrainian officials scrambled to remediate the damage and contain any further disaster, the world became more and more aware of what had transpired in Chernobyl. This was despite the fact that the Soviet government deliberately tried to interrupt information provided to the international community and downplay the seriousness of the situation. As stated previously, the full extent of the disaster began to be known when scientists located hundreds of kilometers away detected high levels of radiation.

The general public—especially in the so-called "first world"—strongly suspected they were being misled, and the media encouraged this way of thinking. Particularly in the United States, journalists assumed that the Soviets were being deceptive and stated as much on television, radio, and in print.

While the media outlets were not wrong about the lack of transparency on the part of the Soviet Union, they also caused more panic than was probably necessary. Much of their information was also flawed; for example, it was reported that reactor number 3 had also suffered significant damage, but this turned out not to be the case. What was more, the aura of mystery in which this disaster was shrouded deepened the global public's distrust of both government and nuclear power.

It is also important to keep in mind that the United States had recently suffered a disaster of its own. In March of 1979, one of the reactors at the nuclear site Three Mile Island in Pennsylvania suffered a partial meltdown. Luckily, the disaster was relatively contained (at least more so than at Chernobyl), but it created a great deal of anxiety about the safety of nuclear power. When the public saw what happened at Chernobyl, their fears only grew.

Thus, in the aftermath of Chernobyl, nuclear energy came under intense scrutiny around the world. Hundreds of planned nuclear construction projects were halted or canceled in response to hostility from the general public. Also in response to Chernobyl, governments around the world passed new regulations that would make nuclear power plants much more expensive to operate. For that reason, the world's use of nuclear power mostly stagnated.

Chernobyl also caused people around the world to seriously question the ability of the Soviet Union to operate nuclear power plants effectively. While initial reports about the causes of the meltdown were conflicting and not clear, it quickly became apparent that human error was involved in the meltdown. In addition, the media drew attention to the fact that the reactor in question was a uniquely Soviet design not used elsewhere in the world. Especially those in neighboring countries greatly feared the continued operation of nuclear power plants by the Soviets, particularly ones with the RBMK design. As was made clear in the second investigation into the accident (discussed in the next chapter), they were right to worry.

There was widespread fear throughout northern Europe and beyond about how far the contaminated materials could potentially spread. Obviously, people within Ukraine in the immediate area were evacuated, but further away, many wondered what the fallout from the disaster would be. Concerns from the international community about contamination from the meltdown were not misplaced. After all, radioactive particles do not respect national borders. Evidence of contamination was very widespread and typically followed wind and other weather patterns that occurred in the weeks and months following the disaster. These damages are discussed in a later chapter.

It is critically important to put the reactions of the global public and other governments in the context of the Cold War. Even though the Soviet Union was nearing its end, the Cold War had escalated significantly during the early-mid 1980s under U.S. President Ronald Reagan. The competition between the U.S. and the Soviet Union was intense and at one of its peak moments when this disaster occurred, dealing a serious blow to the competency of the Soviet Union on the international stage.

What was more, many people around the world questioned whether the Soviet Union was capable of keeping their vast store of nuclear weapons safe if they could not even protect their nuclear power plants. Could an atomic weapon be accidentally detonated or damaged? People around the world wanted answers as to how this accident happened. Much attention and anticipation surrounded the United Nations' official investigation into Chernobyl, which is the subject of the next chapter.

Chapter Seven

Investigations into the Chernobyl Disaster

"The Agency shall seek to accelerate and enlarge the contribution of atomic energy to peace, health, and prosperity throughout the world."

—Statute of the International Atomic Energy Agency

At a time when everything was seen through the lens of the Cold War, a chief concern for the Soviets was not to appear negligent or inept in their management of nuclear power. Otherwise, they feared, the United States might have ammunition to intervene in their nuclear program by using the United Nations.

The investigations were conducted by the International Atomic Energy Agency's International Nuclear Safety Advisory Group (INSAG), which had been formed just a year before the meltdown. This organization conducted two separate investigations that yielded two reports with different findings: INSAG-1 in 1987 and INSAG-7 in 1992.

Both are complex documents which are the result of in-depth investigations that involved interviewing hundreds of people and examining a massive amount of documents and data. It also involved complex mathematical and scientific calculations since so much of the machinery was destroyed in the accident. INSAG-1 was released in September 1986 and placed the blame for the accident on improper safety practices and the actions of the people who operated the reactor. The safety failures were many and on several levels. For one thing, as we have seen, several key safety functions were turned off at the time of the accident. Communication was insufficient, the test itself was poorly planned and executed, and safety checks were not conducted regularly or thoroughly enough.

After the conclusion of the first investigation, the Soviet Union held a criminal trial in which five men were sentenced to terms in labor camps for their roles in the disaster. The first of these men was Anatoly Dyatlov, the deputy chief engineer on duty during the day of the accident. He was sentenced to ten years. Also sentenced to ten years was the chief engineer, Nikolai Fomin, and the plant director at the time, Viktor Bryukhanov.

Lesser plant officials who had a role in running reactor 4 on the day of the disaster were also sentenced to labor camp terms. Boris Rogozhin, the shift director at the time of the disaster, received five years in a Soviet labor camp. The reactor 4 chief at the time, Aleksandr Kovalenko, received a three-year sentence. Finally, a government inspector, Yuri Laushkin, received two years. Three more men were indicted, but they passed away before they could be prosecuted for their roles in what happened at Chernobyl.

Several years later, though, in 1992, INSAG-7 reached different conclusions. While INSAG-7 still acknowledged the role that poor safety practices played in the disaster, it placed the majority of the blame for the disaster on the design of the reactor itself. Specifically, the control rods were critically flawed, and the reactor had a large positive void coefficient of reactivity, making it dangerously unstable at low power levels. Remember, Soviet scientists designed and built these reactors, and they were unique to power plants in the Soviet Union.

However, by this time in 1992, the Berlin Wall had fallen and the Soviet Union had broken up. Therefore, these conclusions were somewhat less damning.

It was actually the fall of the Soviet Union that allowed this reinvestigation. Some of the software used to calculate the events had improved, but the chief difference between INSAG-1 and INSAG-7 (and the reason why the investigation was reopened in the first place) was the declassification of documents related to Chernobyl. In the interim, the KGB declassified several documents that revealed shortcuts during construction and failures in the design that were not available at the time of the first investigation.

While the International Atomic Energy Agency conducted these investigations, people in Ukraine, the Soviet Union (and later Russia), and surrounding areas were working on dealing with the impact of the disaster at Chernobyl Nuclear Power Plant. In the next chapter, we'll take a look at what this entailed.

Chapter Eight

The Impact of the Chernobyl Disaster

"Chernobyl is like the war of all wars. There's nowhere to hide. Not underground, not underwater, not in the air."

—Svetlana Alexievich, *Voices from Chernobyl: The Oral History of a Nuclear Disaster*

The disaster at the Chernobyl Nuclear Power Plant had long-reaching impacts in several areas. First and foremost, it affected many people, especially those living in Pripyat and other nearby cities and towns at the time. It also affected the natural environment, releasing a catastrophic amount of radioactive material into the atmosphere that caused damage near to and far from the site of the disaster. Finally, it also caused a global crisis for nuclear energy, prompting people worldwide to question its safety.

It is somewhat difficult to ascertain the extent of the human damage. Certainly, we know that at least 31 people perished in the first few months after the disaster, and more than 230 suffered acute radiation poisoning. Since then, an additional 15 people have died from thyroid cancer directly tied to the Chernobyl disaster. Experts estimate that at least 4,000 other cases of cancer may have resulted because of radiation poisoning caused by Chernobyl, but that number only represents the people who were in the immediate area on the day of the disaster or who participated in the remediation before the reactor was encased. Another study conducted by Greenpeace placed that number between 10,000-200,000 deaths by 2004 because of the disaster, which is a staggering number. In addition, 18,000 Ukrainian children received treatment in Cuba for their exposure to radioactivity in the years after the disaster.

Again, the data needed to calculate these numbers is hard to compile. By the year 2000, approximately 3.5 million people were receiving government benefits of some kind because of exposure to radiation (there were approximately 5 million people proven to be exposed in total). In addition, fears about radiation exposure caused a surge of abortions in Europe. Pregnant women in Scandinavia and even as far away as Greece elected to abort their fetuses in the aftermath of Chernobyl rather than risk delivering a baby suffering from radiation exposure. A 1987 article published in the *Journal of Nuclear Medicine* placed the estimated number of abortions directly tied to Chernobyl at 150,000.

The accident also caused severe and immediate damage in the areas around the plant. An entire forest located downwind from the power plant withered and died within a matter of weeks. Horses on an island in the Pripyat River died when their thyroids broke down from radiation exposure. Other animals in the area also died out or stopped reproducing because of radiation exposure. In the aftermath of the Chernobyl disaster, several dangerous elements were released into the atmosphere, and some of them had half-lives of more than 20 or 30 years, which means that they may have only recently expired.

Chernobyl affected land in far-away places as well, particularly high ground and mountainous areas as far away as Norway and the United Kingdom. In Norway, as recently as 2018, animals intended for slaughter had high doses of radiation from grazing on land contaminated by the Chernobyl accident more than 30 years prior. The United Kingdom prohibited grazing on high ground that was exposed to radioactive materials, and they have only recently begun to allow it again. In Germany in 2010, a small percentage of slaughtered wild boar showed heightened levels of radiation which have been linked back to Chernobyl.

The Chernobyl meltdown also caused a huge disruption in the supply of food for people in Ukraine and the Soviet Union. Much fertile farmland and grazing land had to be shut down completely in the aftermath while the government scrambled to assess the damage. Millions of people relied on food and foodstuff produced in these regions, and replacements had to come from somewhere. Therefore, the Soviet Union was forced to import a massive amount of safe food.

Outside of the human and environmental impact, perhaps the biggest outcome of the Chernobyl Disaster was the immediate and extreme shift in public opinion about nuclear energy. People worldwide watched the events in the U.S.S.R. in absolute horror and became incredibly fearful of the nuclear reactors in their regions. As discussed in the previous chapter, this fear and widespread outrage became the catalyst for the decommission of many nuclear reactors around the world.

In particular, there was widespread fear directed squarely at the Soviet Union and their presumably lax safety practices. After the first investigation concluded and news of the outcome spread, people outside of the Soviet Union (in Europe in particular) began protesting and calling for them to shut down their nuclear energy program entirely. Exacerbating this outrage, opponents of the Soviet Union, particularly the U.S. and the U.K., emphasized the lack of safety and sloppiness of that program in order to further demonstrate their own superiority (even though the United States experienced the Three Mile Island incident only a few years prior). It is difficult to ascertain what effect Chernobyl and the international response had on the looming end of the Soviet Union, but it's safe to say that it didn't help.

International efforts to repair some of this damage—both human and environmental—have been ongoing. In some ways, they became easier in the late 1980s when the Soviet Union was dismantled. In 1991, the United Nations created the Chernobyl Trust Fund from their Office for the Coordination of Humanitarian Affairs. Since that time, it has helped many of the victims impacted by the disaster rebuild their lives, receive medical care, and more. Separate from this, the United Nations also established the Chernobyl Shelter Fund in 1997 and the Chernobyl Recovery and Development Programme in 2003, both aimed at making the land around the plant inhabitable and safe.

Today, many of these efforts are ongoing. Estimates about when the land will be inhabitable by humans again vary widely. Ukrainian government officials say approximately 300 years (they have maintained this number since 2011), while Greenpeace estimated in 2016 that it would be tens of thousands of years. In 2011, Ukraine opened the 30-kilometer exclusion zone around the plant to tourists, and since then, thousands have come to see the site of so much destruction and suffering.

Chapter Nine

Chernobyl Remembered

"That's how it was in the beginning. We didn't just lose a town, we lost our whole lives."

—Svetlana Alexievich, *Voices from Chernobyl: The Oral History of a Nuclear Disaster*

Chernobyl has loomed like a dark cloud in the memory of the entire world since that fateful April day in 1986. Once again, one of the most important aspects of the memory of the Chernobyl Disaster was the decommissioning of many nuclear power facilities worldwide, as well as the almost immediate halting of the construction of new plants. To this day, this single event casts an incredibly long shadow over nuclear power, one that all of its benefits cannot overshadow.

Whenever any issues have arisen within the field of nuclear power, the memory of Chernobyl is summoned as proof that it is unsafe. It also stokes fears among the public of what could happen. These fears have proven to be not completely unfounded, either. In 2011, a massive earthquake and tsunami caused a Level 7 nuclear disaster at the Fukushima Daiichi Nuclear Power Plant in Okuma, Japan. In the decade following Fukushima, United Nations and Japanese officials have used evidence gathered in the aftermath of Chernobyl to respond more effectively this time around.

Perhaps one of the oddest ways of remembering Chernobyl has been the strange fascination of people with its site, as well as the abandoned city of Pripyat. As we already discussed, the city of Pripyat was hurriedly evacuated on April 27, 1986. Residents fled for their lives in panic and haste, and fears of radioactivity kept them away for many years. This meant that much of the landscape of the city, including homes, shops, restaurants, schools, and more, remained eerily preserved exactly as they appeared on that terrifying day.

Today, Pripyat has become something of a fascination for people from around the world and is a relatively popular tourist site. Several Ukrainian companies take curious visitors on tours of the city, which began in 2011 when the Ukraine opened the exclusion zone. While concerns remain about whether it is safe to do so, studies have shown that the current levels of radiation do not exceed safe limits for short periods of time.

Chernobyl continues to fascinate in other ways, as well. In 2019, HBO released a historical drama miniseries based on the disaster. It is now streaming on Amazon Prime and has been seen by millions of viewers.

Amazingly, Chernobyl was not closed immediately after the disaster. The remaining reactors continued to operate for several years. This continued operation was not without incident, either. In 1991, a fire broke out in reactor two, which precipitated its official decommission. The entire plant was finally closed for good in December 2000, although some experts still think the reactors pose a threat to the world today.

Conclusion

The Chernobyl Disaster shook the faith of the people of the world in the safe use of nuclear power. It also caused an incredible amount of damage to the environment within Ukraine and as far away as Norway and the United Kingdom. Most importantly, it claimed dozens of lives in the immediate aftermath, and perhaps thousands more in the years that have followed.

Chernobyl was shrouded in myth and mystery for many years. The two separate investigations conducted by the International Nuclear Safety Advisory Group reached two very different conclusions, as discussed in chapter seven. The first placed the blame definitively on the plant scientists and government nuclear officials; their lack of preparation, proper safety, and lack of transparency led to the disaster. When very different conclusions were reached a few years later, after the collapse of the Soviet Union, that exacerbated the suspicions held by some. Fascination with Chernobyl has made the site of the disaster into a relatively popular, albeit macabre, tourist destination.

Chernobyl—and the more recent disaster at Fukushima—are held up by many environmental advocates and other organizations as proof of the danger of nuclear power. They're not entirely wrong. The damage from both of these incidents is still felt in places near and far. It is left to be seen whether the site at Fukushima will elicit the same degree of fascination in the years to come.

Chernobyl is important for a number of reasons. It changed the world's impression of nuclear power and created incredible distrust in its safety. It also undermined the technological and scientific credibility of the Soviet Union. The Chernobyl disaster remains one of only two nuclear disasters rated at a seven (maximum severity) on the International Nuclear Event Scale. It is doubtful that this incident and its aftermath will fade from popular memory anytime soon.

Bibliography

Alexievich, S. (2015). *Voices from Chernobyl: The Oral History of a Nuclear Disaster.*

Higginbotham, A. (2019). *Midnight in Chernobyl: The Untold Story of the World's Greatest Nuclear Disaster.*

Leatherbarrow, A., and Petrey, E. (2016). *Chernobyl 01:23:40: The Incredible True Story of the World's Worst Nuclear Disaster.*

Mahaffey, J. (2014). *Atomic Accidents: A History of Nuclear Meltdowns and Disasters: From the Ozark Mountains to Fukushima.*

Plokhy, S. (2018). *Chernobyl: The History of a Nuclear Catastrophe.*

United States Office of Nuclear Energy. https://www.energy.gov/

World Nuclear Association. (2021). "Chernobyl Accident, 1986." https://world-nuclear.org/information-library/safety-and-security/safety-of-plants/chernobyl-accident.aspx

Made in the USA
Middletown, DE
12 November 2021

52259923R00035